FIFA World Cup

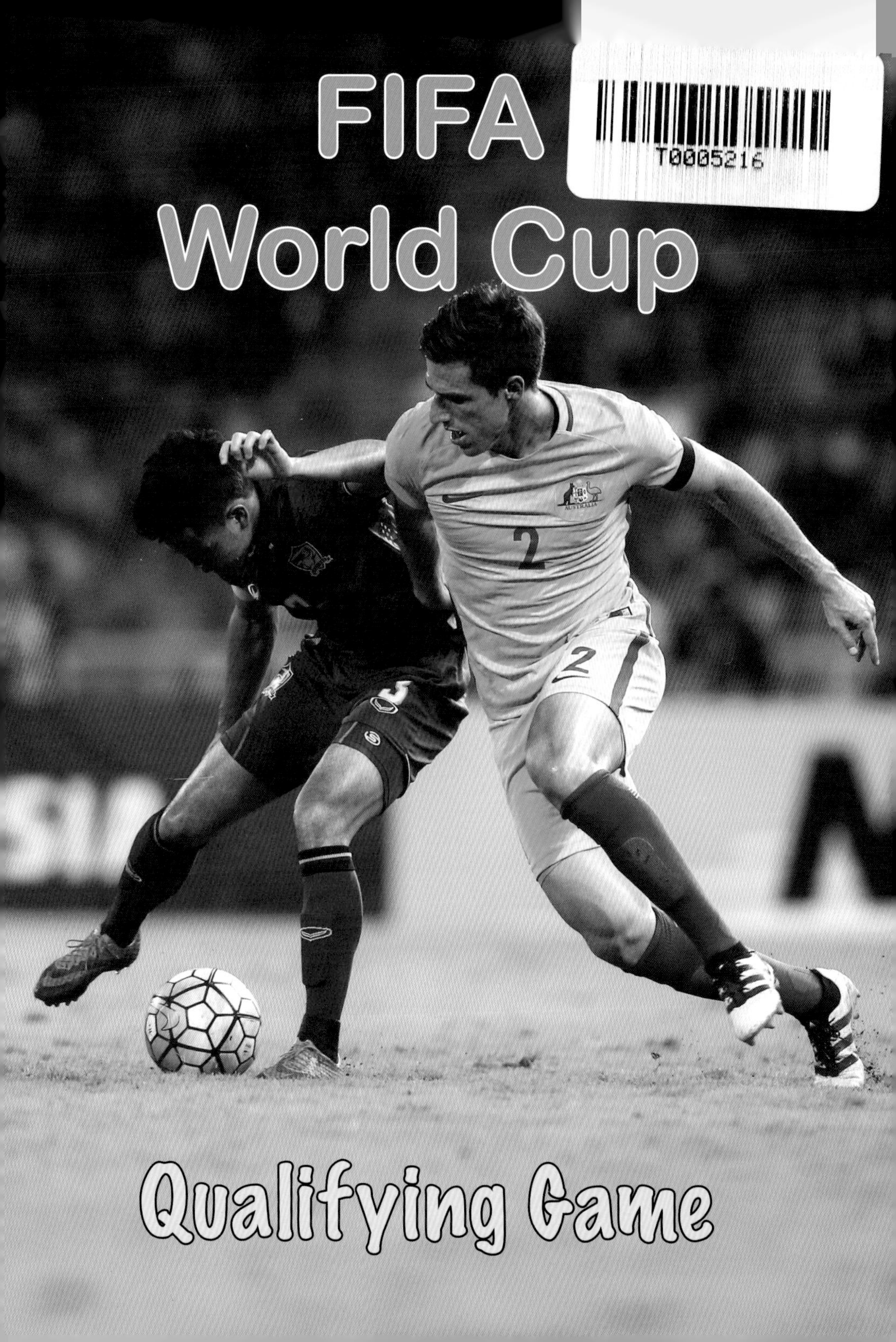

Qualifying Game

This is my team.

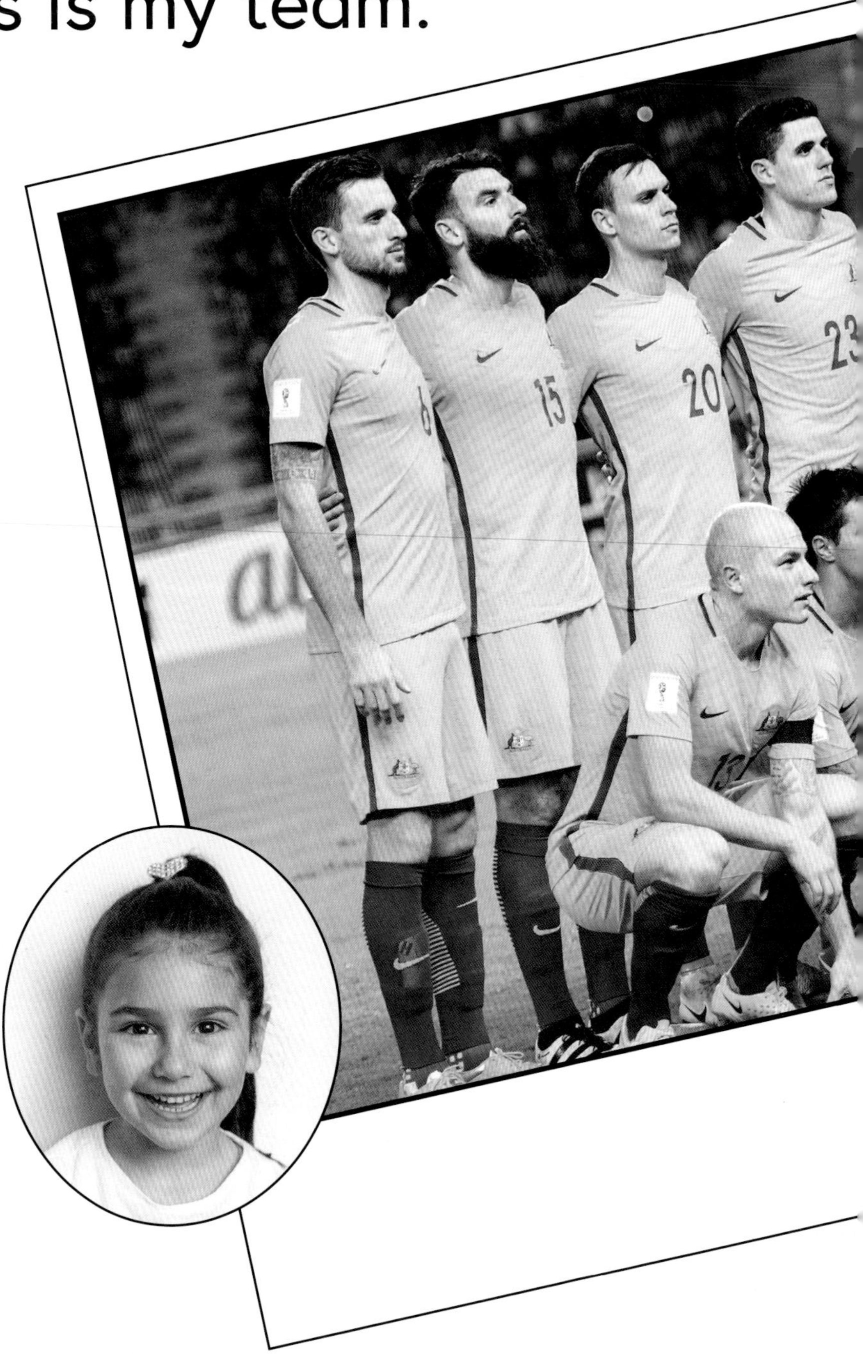

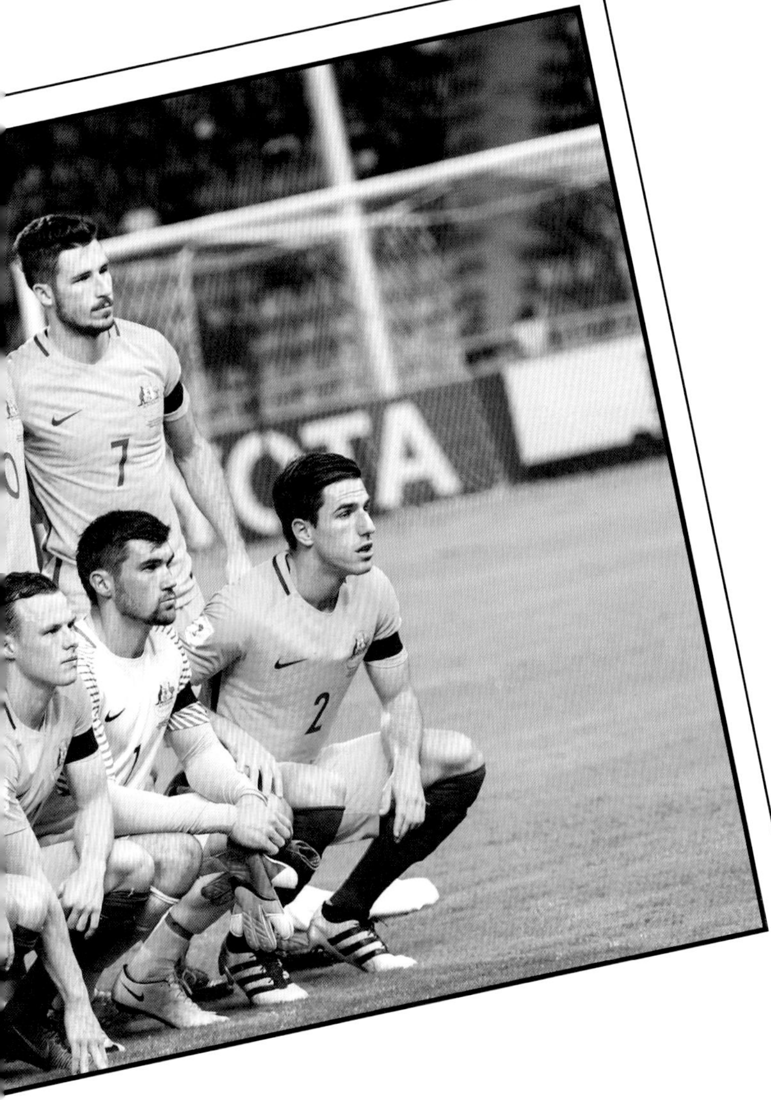

This is my team.

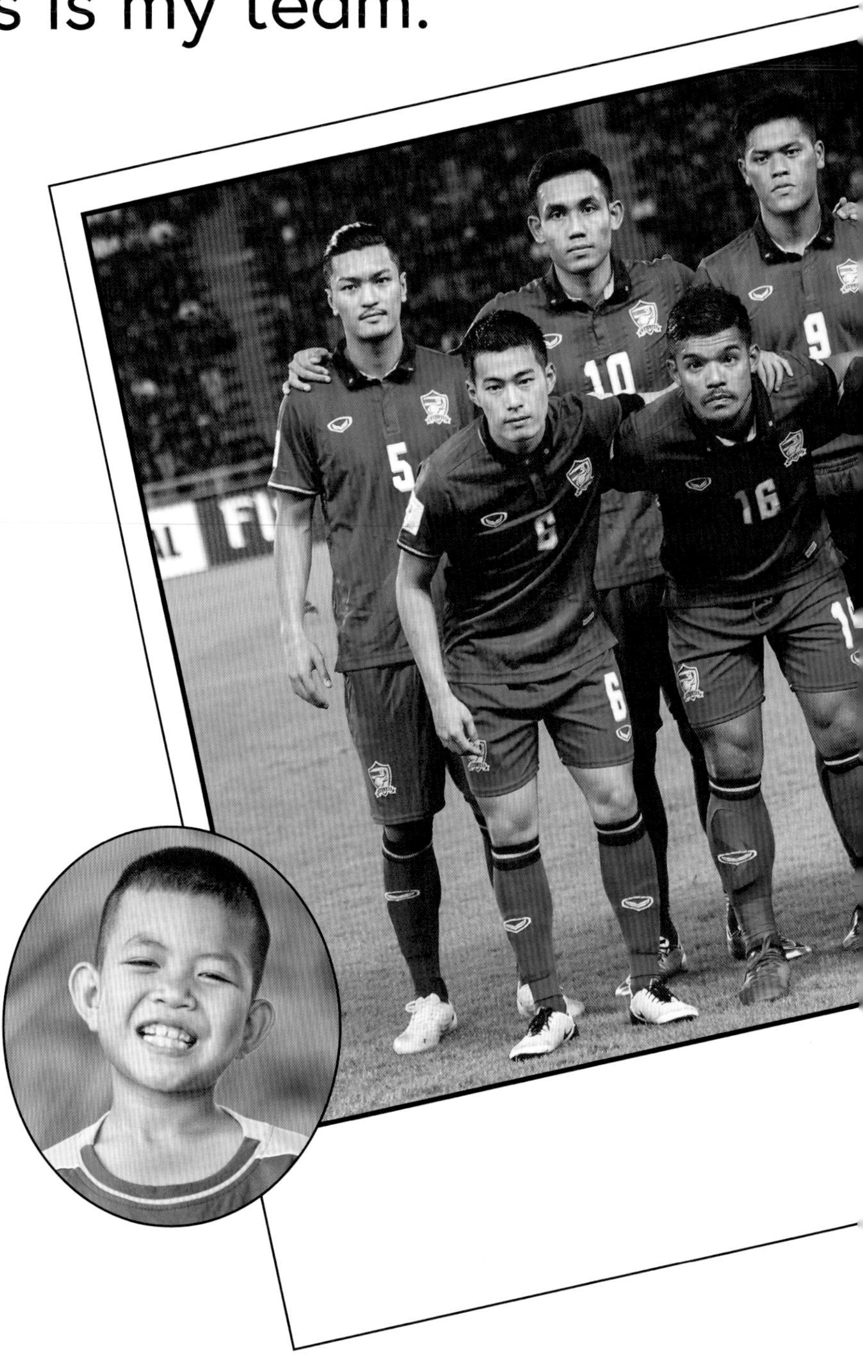

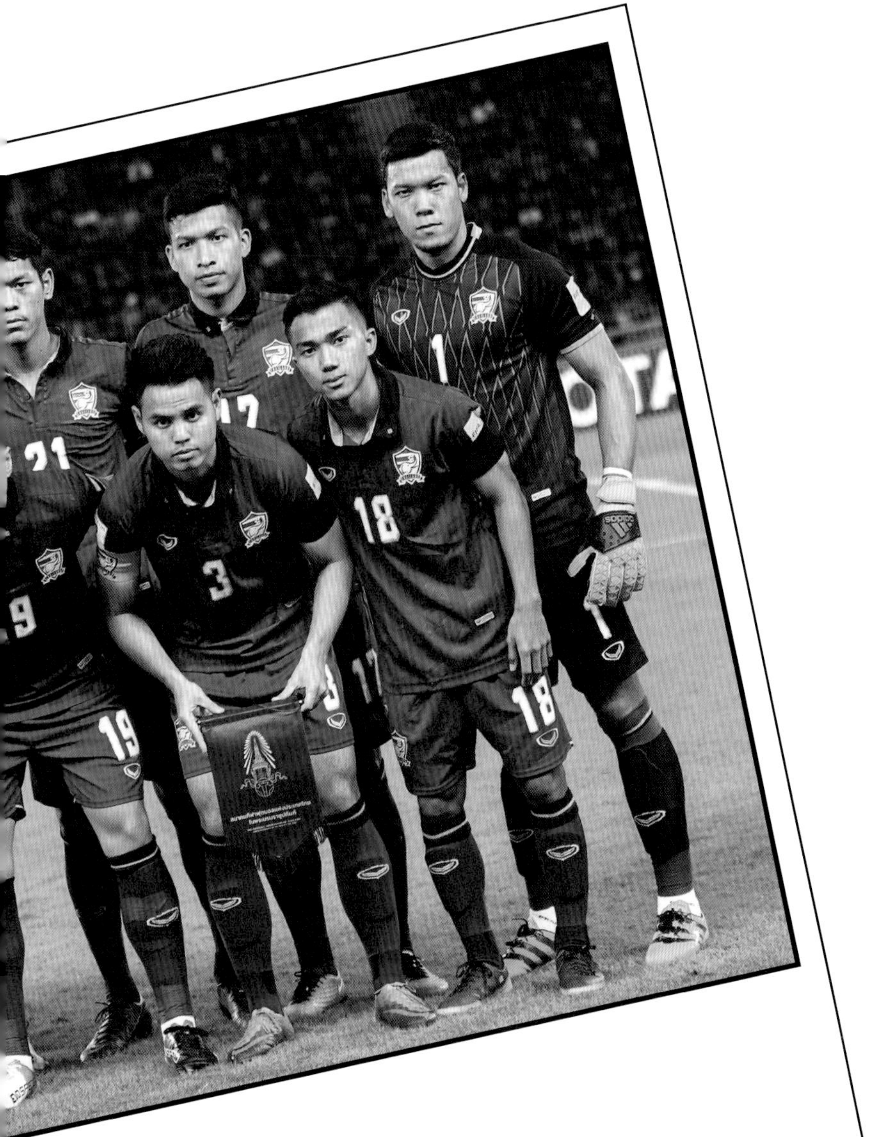

My team runs.

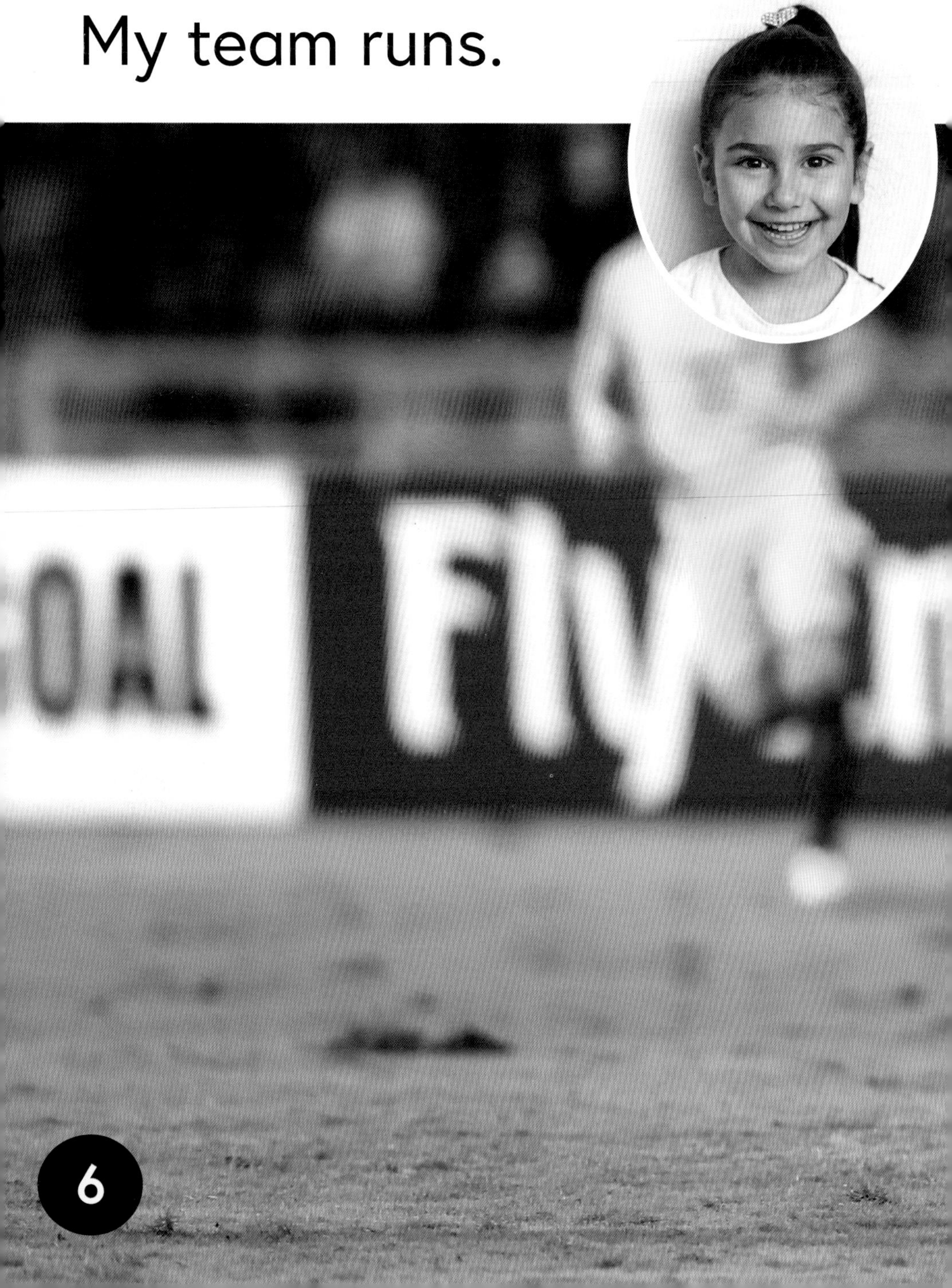

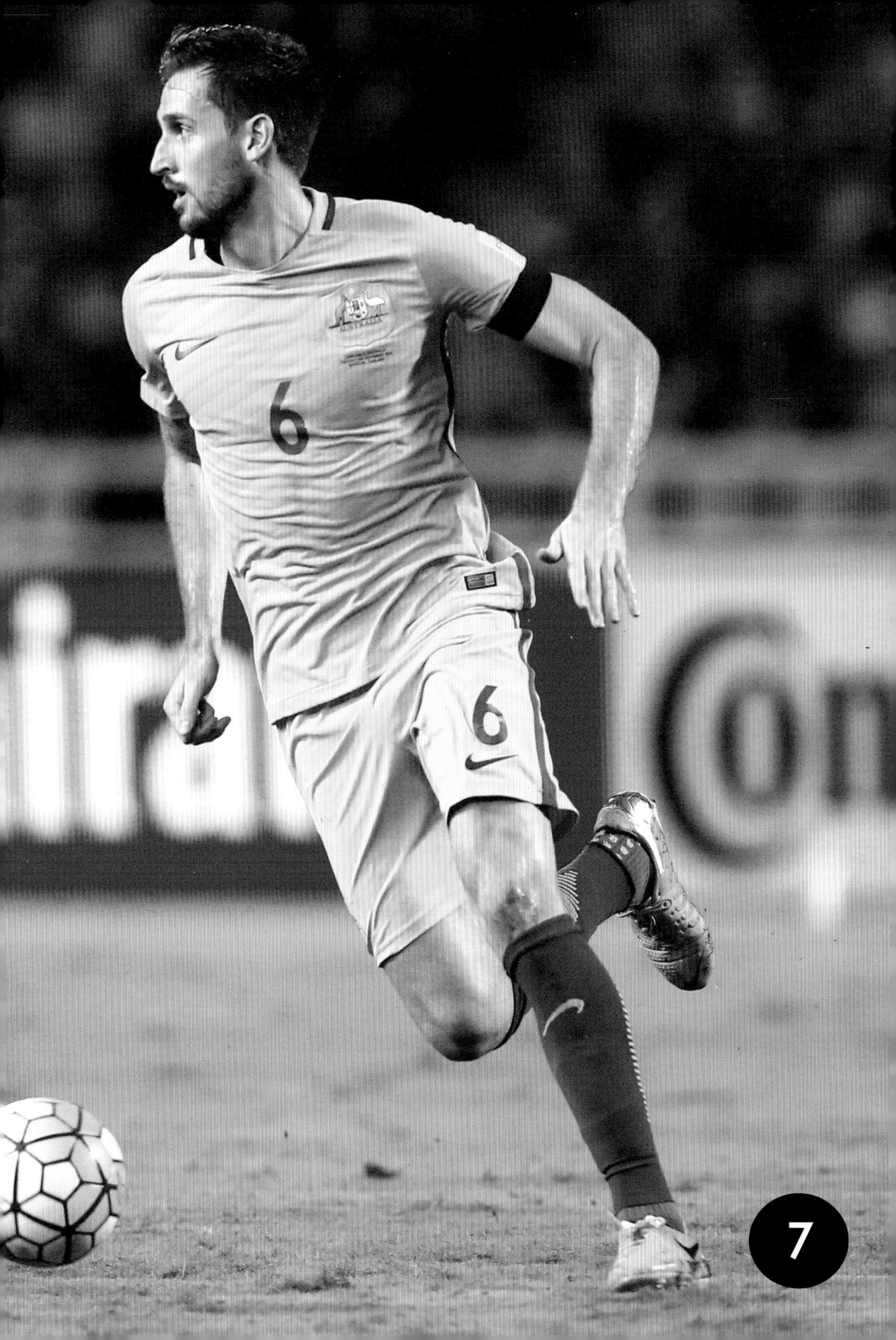

My team jumps.

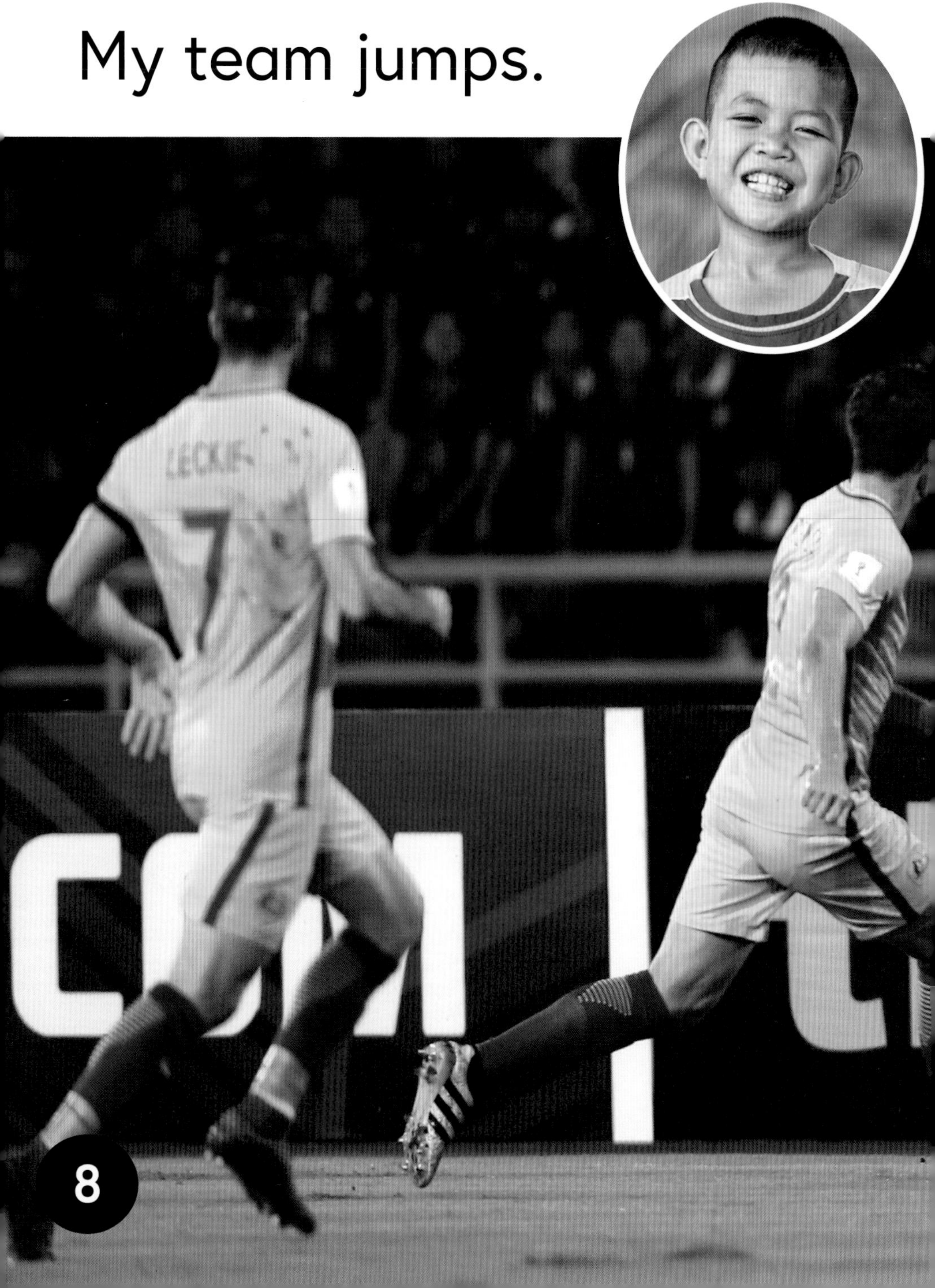

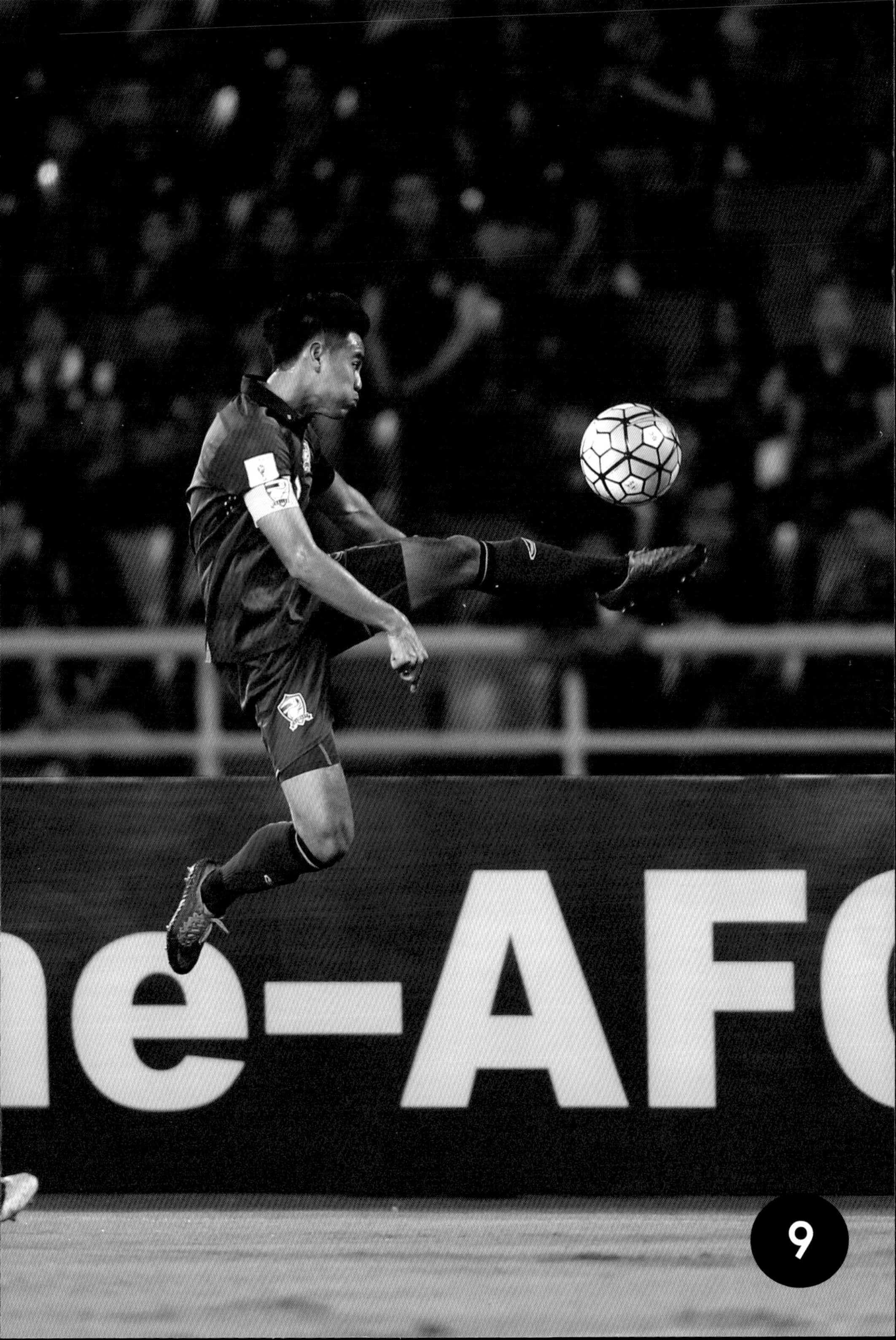
ne-AF

My team kicks.

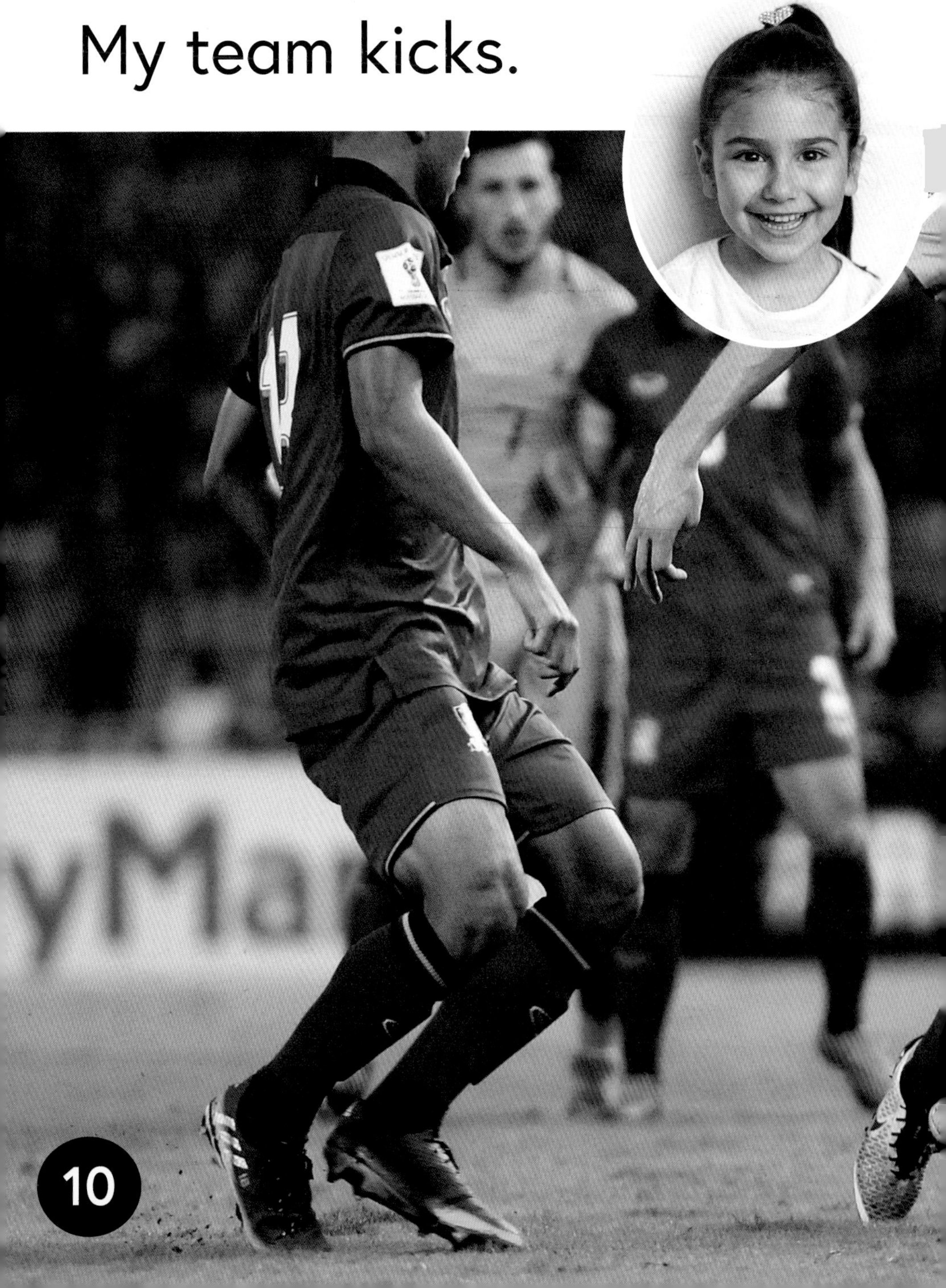

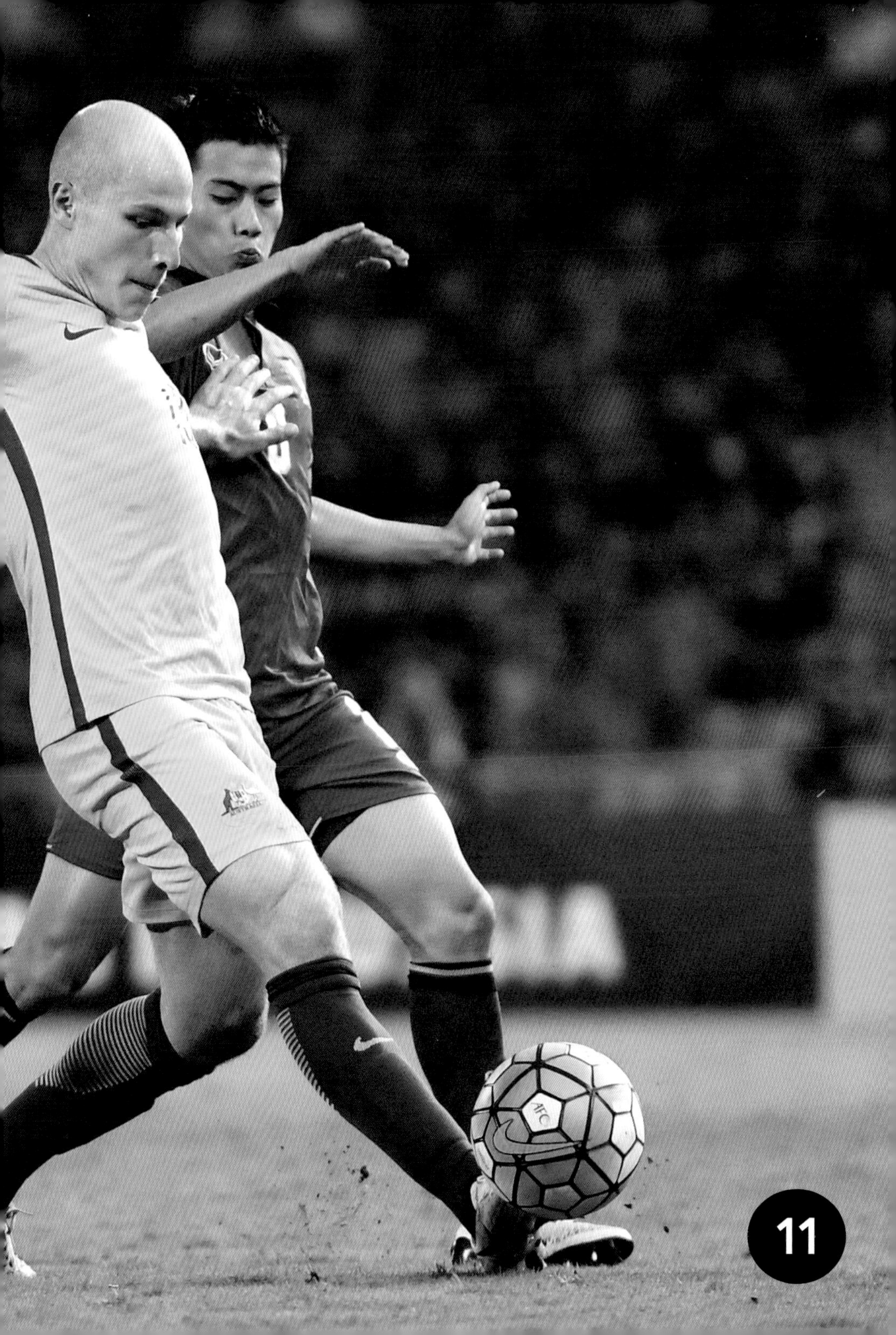

My team slides.

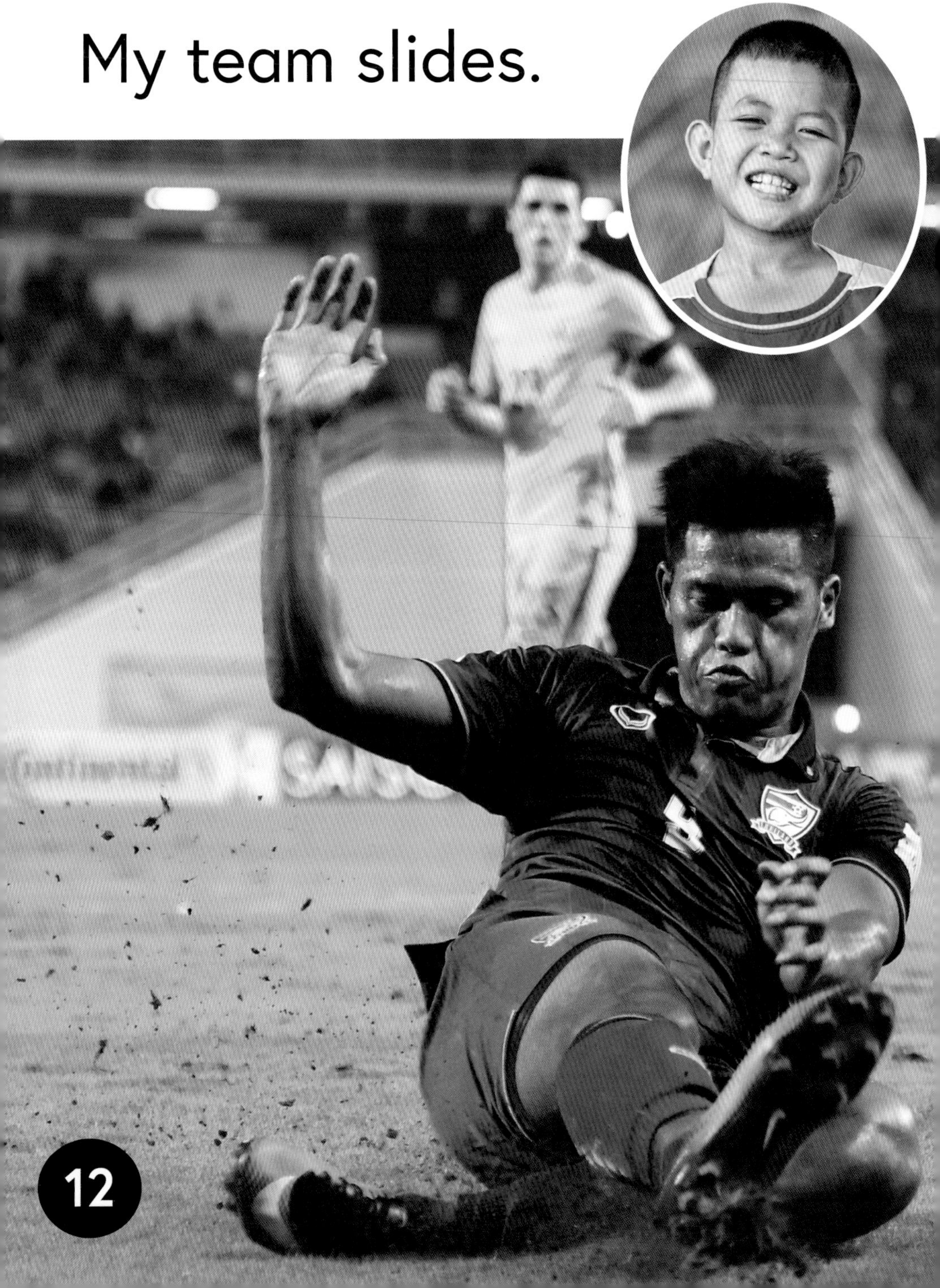

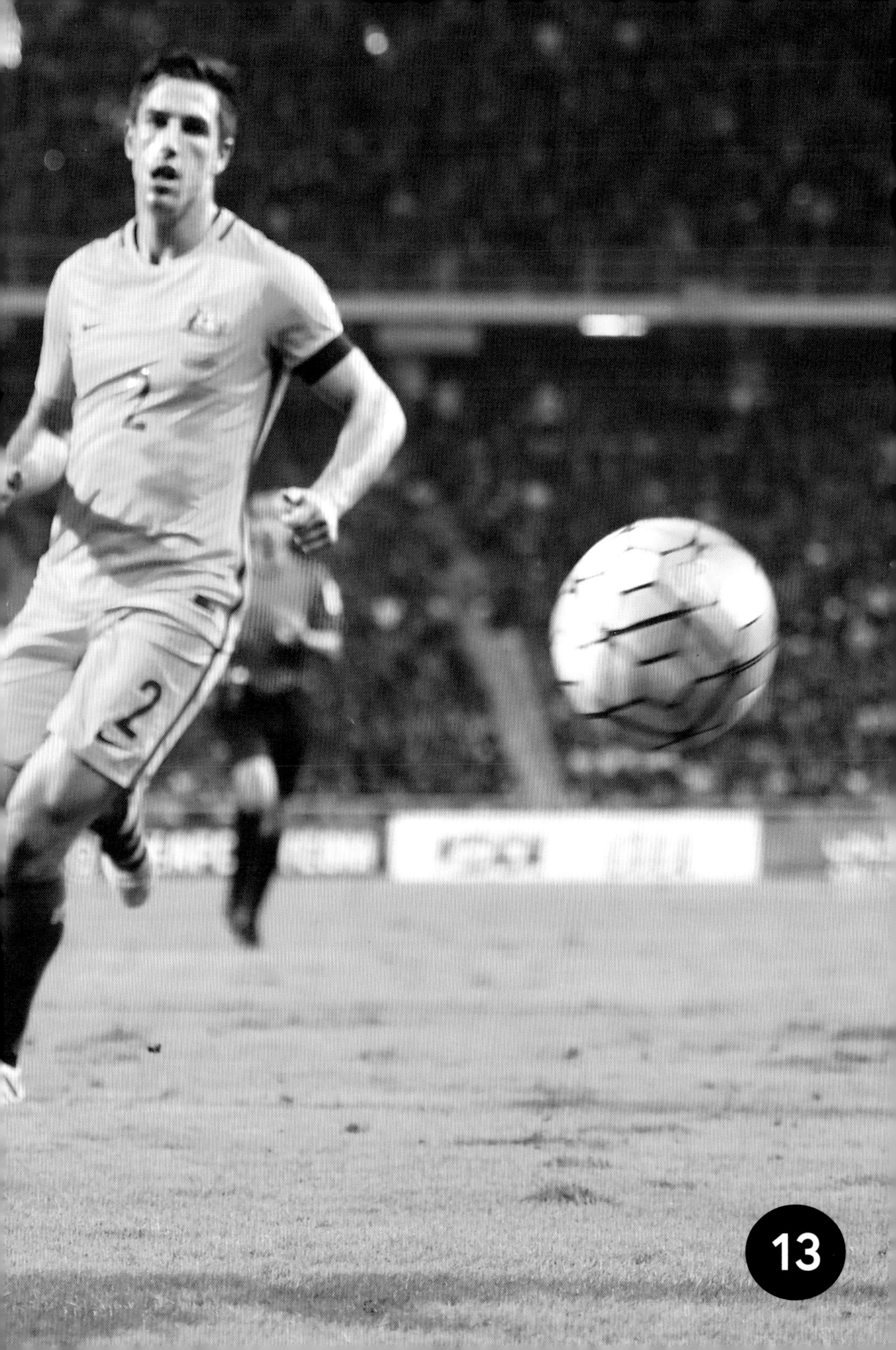

My team scores.

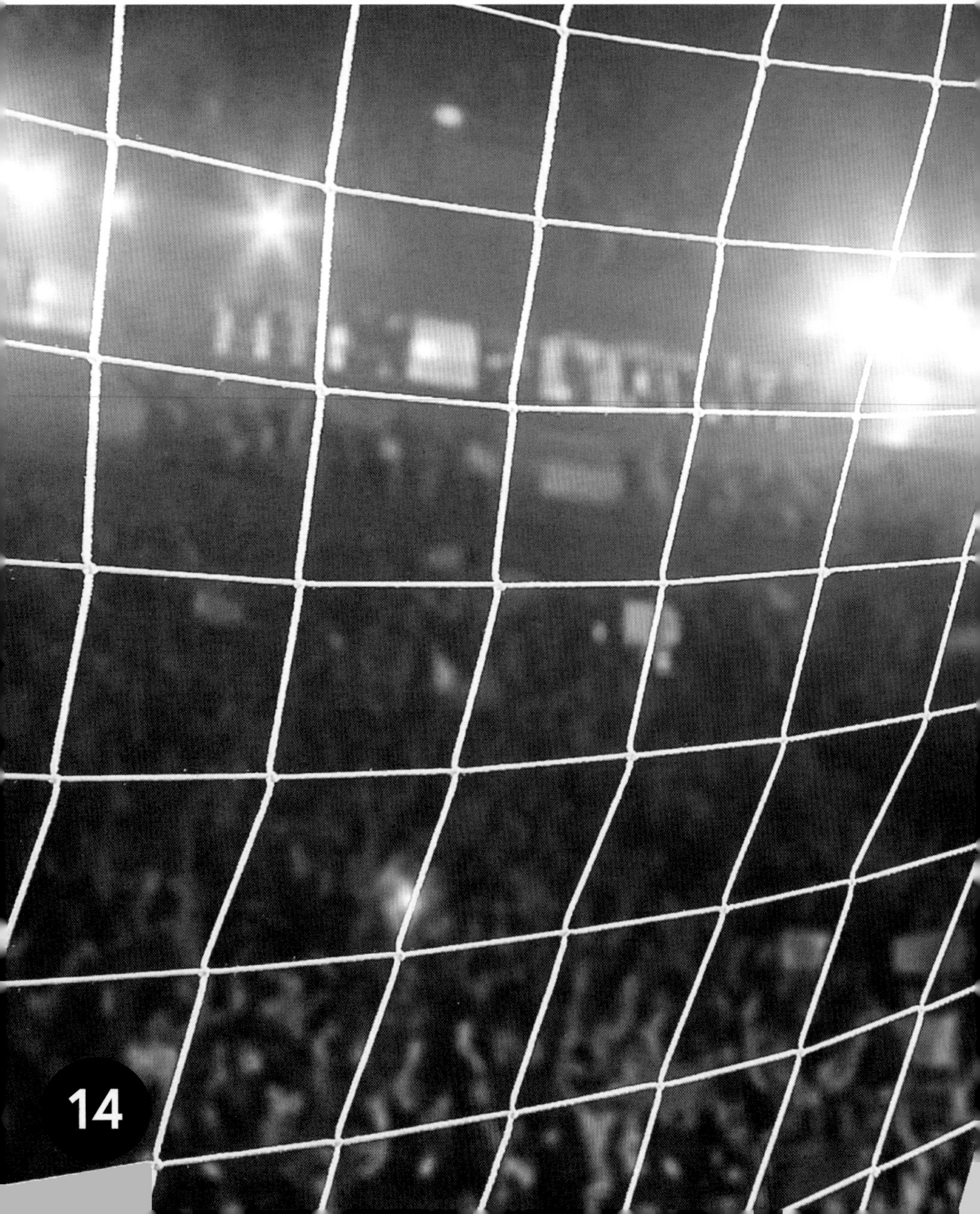

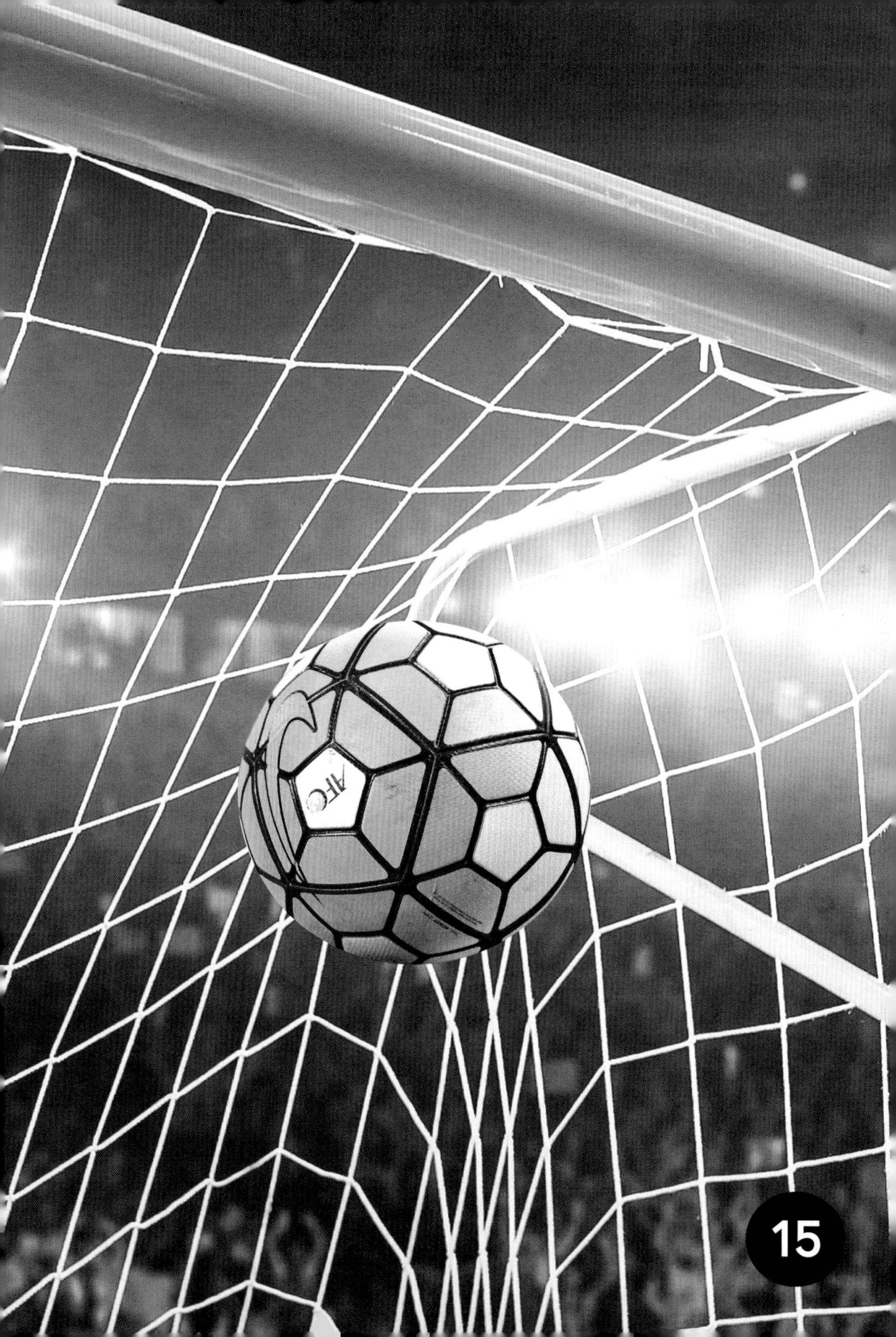

My team wins!

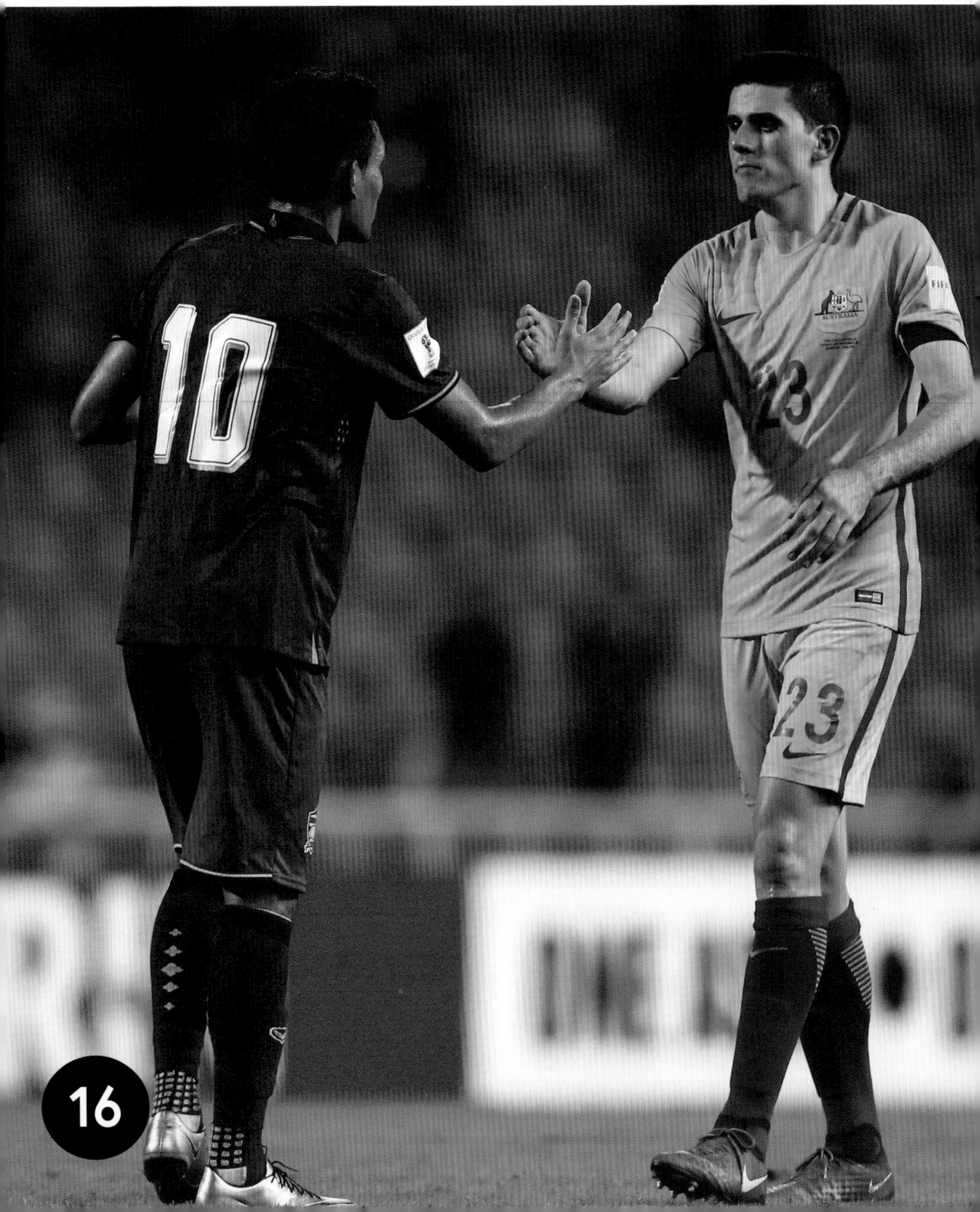